FINDING HAPPINESS AND PURPOSE IN LIFE

Books edited by Arpita Mitra

'Liberate Your Mind': Life Lessons from Sri Ramakrishna

FINDING HAPPINESS AND PURPOSE IN LIFE

Timeless Wisdom From Around the World

Edited by Arpita Mitra

ALEPH

ALEPH BOOK COMPANY
An independent publishing firm
promoted by ***Rupa Publications India***

First published in India in 2023
by Aleph Book Company
7/16 Ansari Road, Daryaganj
New Delhi 110 002

ISBN: 978-93-93852-96-0

1 3 5 7 9 10 8 6 4 2

Printed in India

Let noble thoughts come to us from all sides.

—Rig Veda

Contents

INTRODUCTION

This anthology was conceived out of the desire to bring to the reader the wealth of wisdom that exists in the world since ancient times—this wisdom will help us find our way in the world, through its complications and sufferings. While the lion's share of aphorisms has been collected from the diverse traditions of India, all that is noble and wise in other cultures have also found their place in this anthology. The company of the great minds of the world will elevate our spirit above the mundane and assuage our pain arising from loss, unfulfilled desires, and so on. They are considered great by virtue of their ability to transcend the finitude of human existence and actualize its ultimate potential. Although the bulk of the aphorisms presented here are spiritual, they do not call for belief in any dogmas related to any particular religion. They do not even ask or expect us to believe in a particular kind of god, or to believe in God at all! These sagacious sayings are an invitation for the human mind to soar high in the realm of contemplation, demanding no blind belief but only critical self-reflection.

The human condition is such that, beyond a point, fundamental and deep questions are bound to arise in the thoughtful person. What is the meaning of life? Why do we suffer? How can we be happy? These are questions shared by both the common man on the street and the most profound philosopher. Most individuals desire one thing—happiness. Thus, the philosopher or the saint is bound to reflect on this question. The only difference is that ordinarily, we seek happiness where it is not to be found. A person with a spiritual bent of mind will discover sooner or later that this happiness exists within him/her, and that in vain does he/she try to look for it outside, much like the misguided deer who does not know that the musk emanates from its own person. It is but natural that we would seek happiness; for we come from happiness, we come from joy unbound. So says the Vedanta, which describes our real nature as 'sat-chit-ananda', that is, existence, consciousness, and bliss. Philosophies like Buddhism and Jainism that do not accept the authority of the Vedas also call it a grave mistake to consider ourselves as merely a combination of body and mind. If we are essentially bliss unconditional in essence, why do we suffer? What ails humanity? IGNORANCE—is what they would say in unison. It is ignorance of our real nature, it is ignorance of reality itself that makes us suffer. It is a mistake to think suffering is thrust upon us. We *choose* suffering. This realization itself is emancipatory because it equally makes happiness, contentment, and peace a choice.

Our greatest fear is the fear of death. We know death to be a certain fact of existence, yet we live as if we are going to live forever. Hence, we amass wealth, and try to enjoy worldly life to the hilt. It is precisely this that leads us farther and farther away from happiness, for true happiness is only to be found in contentment. It is contentment that leads us to peace, eventually helping us see clearly the finitude of worldly existence and cultivate compassion for all. Thereby, we abandon all efforts at meeting selfish ends. There is no harm in the enjoyment of worldly life; but that enjoyment must be tempered with the knowledge of the eventuality of life, that is, death. This will make us less anxious, and lead to living life in the present moment and with the awareness that neither pleasure nor pain is meant to last forever. Once the mind becomes calm, it sets out on the quest for our true identity, our true purpose in life. Whether or not one aspires for spiritual emancipation, the knowledge of the impermanence of life, of pleasure and pain, and everything else with it, is at least useful to help navigate the maze of life. If we are willing and courageous, this knowledge will eventually lead us to freedom instead of confining us in the throes of anxiety. Peace and bliss lie beyond the duality of pleasure and pain. Living a life that is in consonance with this truth will help us achieve true freedom of the mind. Wise is one who takes advantage of every adversity that presents itself for the cause of self-development.

Apart from joy, it is also freedom we seek in the heart of our hearts—freedom to follow our path to self-development (one size does not fit all!), freedom from limitations and sorrow. Once again, we seek freedom because we have come from freedom—a perfect state of unconditioned existence without any limitations. The ordinary notion of freedom is, however, conditioned by our finite existence. By freedom, we usually think of freedom to do whatever we wish, even if our wish flies in the face of the laws of nature! This is not freedom, but another form of slavery—we are being held captive by our instincts. The secret of attaining freedom is to go beyond nature. Nature governs us through our body and our sense organs that crave the experience of pleasure. Bodily urges dictate the course of life for the most part of humankind. We need to reflect on the truth that we are not bodies, but an entity merely dwelling in this body, taking this body as its habitation for the singular purpose that ultimately, we will find our way back to our source, or real nature. True freedom is not freedom *of* the senses, but *from* the senses. This has been the ultimate message of Indian spiritual traditions. True freedom is freedom from all vices and being established in our real nature that is pure and blissful. These are not mere beliefs or dogmas, but the realizations of seekers and are evident to those who try to lead a life of self-reflection.

The spiritual might seem out of reach for many, as it demands subtle perception—perception of something whose presence is not evident to our sense organs. We cannot see or touch our inner being. However, what is near at hand is the ethical. The law of cause and effect demands us to be moral. There is a relationship between the ethical and the spiritual. While eventually the spiritual transcends the duality of good and evil, the ethical is a necessary first step to the spiritual. Spirituality cannot come to one who does not possess sound moral conduct. Thus, all streams of spiritual thought have laid great emphasis on moral practice as a precondition for spiritual attainment. For instance, the *Yoga Sutra* of Patanjali at the very outset lays down the prescription for moral conduct through its concept of 'yama' which is the first limb of Ashtanga Yoga ('Yoga with Eight Limbs'). It is also the most difficult to perfect. One who has mastered this level can easily accomplish the subsequent ones.

What constitutes moral conduct? Truthfulness, non-injury, forbearance, compassion, non-covetousness, and generosity are some of the fundamental virtues. All traditions lay great emphasis on the practice of truthfulness. If we wish to uncover the truth about our own existence, we need to make truth our constant companion and friend. However, it is equally important that truth should be expressed in a way that is not hurtful to anyone. The habit of finding fault with others tarnishes one's own mind. The instinctive reaction of retaliating to injury is to be abjured under all circumstances; else, the cycle of cause (injury) and effect (suffering) will be perpetuated. Non-injury or non-violence should not only be of the body but also of the mind and speech; that is, one should not hurt anyone physically, think evil thoughts about that person in one's mind, or utter hurtful words. All evil actions are to be refrained from at the physical and mental level as well as at the level of speech. Whatever creates greater sense of separateness and division between human beings is evil. In reality, all of us are connected to each other as we come from the same source. Whether we choose to call this common source 'God' or the 'Big Bang' or something else is unimportant; the fact remains that the entire universe has a common origin. Thus, anything that promotes this feeling of oneness is a virtue, and anything that creates a greater feeling of separation is vice. Jealousy and fear arise from this sense of separateness. If we felt oneness with someone, that person's happiness would be our happiness, and we would not be jealous. Similarly, we would never fear someone with whom we feel oneness. Our natural mode of existence is that we perceive ourselves and everybody else as bodies. This creates and fosters a sense of separateness. This feeling of separateness exacerbates vice, and vice in turn exacerbates the feeling of separateness. So continues the vicious cycle. In order to break the chain, virtue is to be practised. Virtue fosters forbearance and the feeling of oneness.

Just as all human beings desire happiness and freedom, all of us equally desire love. The saint would say we have come from love! So, it is but natural that we would seek love. It is in love alone that human life seeks fulfilment. However, it is not easy to love. Love demands complete self-surrender, complete unselfishness with only the desire to serve the loved one. Love and fear cannot cohabit.

Finally, love is always unconditional. It is sufficient unto itself; it does not seek any return.

Anger is the bane of humanity. But what is the root cause of anger? While there can be myriad reasons for anger, the root cause can usually be reduced to one or two related factors. Anger definitely emanates from egotism. But there is another cardinal reason behind anger—attachment. Human life is propelled by two drives: attraction for the pleasurable and the avoidance of painful experiences. All humans desire pleasure, and try to avoid pain. Repeated experiences of pleasure create more desire for pleasure, and that in turn creates attachment to the object or experience of pleasure. On the other hand, the experience of pain creates a feeling of repulsion—we detest anything that can cause the slightest discomfort to us. This attachment and repulsion are called 'raga' (liking) and 'dvesa' (disliking) in Indian traditions.

Attachment is bondage. The Bhagavad Gita says that whenever the desire for enjoying an object to which we are attached is thwarted, it produces anger. Thus, the root cause of anger is desire and attachment. The Gita also elaborates that attachment arises when one thinks about objects of desire. Again, Gautama Buddha was once asked what gives birth to vice. He replied that vice arises from 'liking' and 'disliking', which in turn stem from desire. When asked what gives rise to desire, the Buddha replied, 'It arises...from thinking. When the mind thinks about something, desire arises; when the mind thinks of nothing, desire does not arise.' Thus, Indic traditions give the same verdict on desire. Renunciation is the only way. As the philosopher Bhartrihari says, 'In this life, all is fraught with fear. Renunciation alone is fearless.' Renunciation is nothing but the absence of desire. It does not mean not enjoying; it means not getting attached to enjoyment, that is, neither craving for enjoyment, nor getting upset in the absence of objects of enjoyment. This is a difficult state to attain unless one has initially practised austerity and abstinence. One cannot enjoy and abstain simultaneously. But a person who has an initial practice of abstinence, can remain unattached even while enjoying. Raga and dvesa are the obverse and reverse of the same coin. One who has renounced is one who neither desires nor refuses.

One important component of this journey is service. Unselfishness and the spirit of service are the very essence of religion. As the Saraswati Veena exponent Sufi Hazrat Inayat Khan (1882–1927) puts it, 'The essence of spirituality and mysticism is readiness to serve the person next to us.' Swami Vivekananda (1863–1902) even said, 'Blessed are they whose bodies get destroyed in the service of others.' Again, Swami Ashokananda (1893–1969), the minister-in-charge of the Vedanta Society of Northern California, remarked that 'depth in meditation will not come without quieting the mind', and that 'the mind is quieted best by unselfishness'. In other words, spirituality is not just about external practices; the person who is unselfish is truly spiritual. Such people are truly happy too, because they have transcended the limitations of narrow selfhood and its accompaniments like desire, jealousy, expectations, and so on. And such people are also truly powerful, because all power arises from unselfishness. Indian lore remembers the sage Dadhichi who sacrificed his life in order that his bones could be used to make the invincible Vajra[1] for Indra, who then slayed the demon Vritra with this powerful weapon that symbolizes unselfishness.

These precepts provide us with the know-how to live our lives meaningfully. But is it possible to change deeply ingrained habits, perceptions, and tendencies? Today we talk about the plasticity of the mind. This is putting ancient wisdom into our modern language. The wise of yore were aware that one's nature is formed through repeated actions, which we call habit. In India, we called deep impressions and tendencies created by habit samskaras. If we are habituated to thinking or behaving in a particular way, we'll continue to do so. Soon, it becomes character. Creating new neural pathways signifies changing old patterns and giving the mind new habits and tendencies or samskaras. Everything, right from our primal emotions like fear and anger to sexual attraction, is shaped by habits over a significant period (according to some beliefs, through several births). What

---

[1]Indra's weapon for destroying sin and ignorance.

we call our natural tendency is simply solidified habit. The only way of countering evil or undesirable tendencies is to practice and cultivate the opposite habits. If one wishes to move away from the north, one has to move in the direction of south. Similarly, if one wishes to conquer jealousy, one has to practice sharing; if one wishes to conquer arrogance, one has to practice serving others; in order to counter negative thoughts, one has to cultivate positive thoughts. I hope this anthology will show many such ways of conquering selfishness, greed, fear, anger, and ignorance about our real nature.

Arpita Mitra
July 2023

PEACE

Om shanti, shanti, shanti Om, peace (in me[1]), peace (in nature[2]), peace (in the divine forces[3]).

~Vedic Shanti Mantra

Let me tell you one thing—if you want peace, my dear, do not find fault with others. See only your own faults. Learn to accept everyone as your own, no one is a stranger, my child, the whole world is your own.

~Sri Sarada Devi

The man of prayer will be at peace with himself and with the whole world, the man who goes about the affairs of the world without a prayerful heart will be miserable and will make the world also miserable.

~Mahatma Gandhi

---

[1]To ward off suffering caused by one's own body and mind.

[2]To ward off suffering inflicted by other human beings, animals, and the physical world.

[3]To ward off suffering caused by adversities such as natural calamities, epidemics, and so on.

Surrender your selfishness and you will attain that sinless, calm state of mind, of peace, goodness, and wisdom.

~The Buddha

FAULT-FINDING

Do not speak ill of others, not even of the insect.

~Sri Ramakrishna

People only see faults.
One should be able to see others' qualities.

~Sri Sarada Devi

Human beings are unhappy due to their own faults.
They can be happy only by correcting
their faults themselves.

~Mahavira

In criticizing a person, you are shutting off the most
wonderful truth: that person is God.

~Swami Ashokananda

If only we would stop the practice of finding fault,
fault-free our world would become
by that one single halt!

~Kural

CONTENTMENT

A greedy person is never content; he may have the wealth of the whole world. Contentment is a must to realize God.

~Guru Granth Sahib

There is no quality that equals patience,
and no wealth that equals contentment.

~Sri Sarada Devi

From contentment, unsurpassed happiness is gained.

~Patanjali, Yoga Sutra

Or fame or life, which do you hold more dear?
Or life or wealth, to which would you adhere?
Keep life and lose those other things; keep them and lose your life: which brings sorrow and pain more near?
Thus we may see, who cleaves to fame rejects what is more great; who loves large stores,
gives up the richer state.
Who is content, needs fear no shame.
Who knows to stop, incurs no blame.
From danger free, long live shall he.

~Tao Te Ching

RETALIATION

Anger is favourable to the enemy.
It brings grief to the person (who gets angry) and to his relatives. It defeats the person (who is angry) and ultimately destroys him.

~Mahavira

Enmity is an ill, a grievous ill, to shun.
Shunning it, the world's praise is won.

~Kural

While water cleanses the body, knowledge cleanses the intellect. One's inner being is cleansed by abstaining from hurting others, and the mind is cleansed by truth.

~Baudhayana Dharmasutra

He who calls himself my enemy puts thorns in my way.
I wish for his garden to bloom,
and let all the flowers in that garden be without thorns.

~Hazrat Nizamuddin

When someone says something unkind to you, you may want to retaliate right away. That is where the fight begins. This habitual way of reacting creates a well-worn pathway in your brain.

When you travel a neural pathway over and over again, it becomes a habit. Very often that pathway leads to anger, fear, or craving. One millisecond is enough for you to arrive at the same destination: anger and a desire to punish the person who has dared to make you suffer.

The mind and the brain are plastic in nature. You can change your mind, your brain, and the way you think and feel. With practice, you can create new neural pathways that lead to understanding, compassion, love, and forgiveness. Mindfulness and insight can intervene, redirecting you down a new neural pathway.

~Thich Nhat Hanh

FORGIVENESS

Kindness and forgiveness are the virtues
to be practised to perfection.
When one prays it should be for the salvation of all.
Raise your spirit to a higher level of consciousness.

~*Hazrat Nizamuddin*

Blessed are the merciful,
for they shall obtain mercy.

~*The New Testament*

Forgiveness is the quality of the brave,
not of the cowardly.

~*Mahatma Gandhi*

LOVE

However much we describe and explain love,
when we fall in love we are ashamed of our words.
Explanation by the tongue makes most things clear,
but love unexplained is clearer.
When pen hasted to write,
on reaching the subject of love it split in twain.
When the discourse touched on the matter of love,
pen was broken and paper torn.
In explaining it Reason sticks fast, as an ass in mire;
naught but Love itself can explain love and lovers!
None but the sun can display the sun,
if you would see it displayed, turn not away from it.

~*Rumi*

When love beckons to you, follow him,
though his ways are hard and steep.
And when his wings enfold you, yield to him,
though the sword hidden among his pinions
may wound you.
And when he speaks to you, believe in him,
though his voice may shatter your dreams as the north
wind lays waste the garden.
For even as love crowns you, so shall he crucify you.

Even as he is for your growth, so is he for your pruning. Even as he ascends to your height and caresses your tenderest branches that quiver in the sun, so shall he descend to your roots and shake them in their clinging to the earth.

~Kahlil Gibran

The word 'love' is very difficult to understand;
love never comes until there is freedom.

~Swami Vivekananda

Through loving kindness, everyone and everything can flower again from within.
Jealousy and envy are like toxins,
poisoning you from within.
Let them go, and make room for love.

~Hazrat Sheikh Moinuddin Chishti

You are love. You come from love.
You are made by love.
You cannot cease to love.

~Hazrat Inayat Khan

When other cravings ceased, peace came to me.
I prepared my heart in the pestle of love.
Then emblazoned it and partook of it.
Now if I live or die, it's all the same to me!

~Lal Ded

We see love everywhere in nature. Whatever in society is good and great and sublime is the working out of that love; whatever in society is very bad, nay diabolical, is also the ill-directed working out of the same emotion of love.... It is the same feeling of love, well or ill-directed, that impels one man to do good and give all he has to the poor, while it makes another man cut the throats of his brethren and take away all their possessions. The former loves others as much as the latter loves himself.... Therefore love, the intense longing for association, the strong desire on the part of two to become one—and it may be, after all, of all to become merged in one—is being manifested everywhere in higher or lower forms as the case may be.

~Swami Vivekananda

If I speak with the languages of men and of angels, but don't have love, I have become sounding brass or a clanging cymbal. If I have the gift of prophecy, and know all mysteries and all knowledge, and if I have all faith, so as to remove mountains, but don't have love, I am nothing. If I give away all my goods to feed the poor, and if I give my body to be burned, but don't have love, it profits me nothing.

~The New Testament

Love is patient and is kind. Love doesn't envy. Love doesn't brag, is not proud, doesn't behave itself inappropriately, doesn't seek its own way, is not provoked, takes no account of evil; doesn't rejoice in unrighteousness, but rejoices with the truth; bears all things, believes all things, hopes all things, and endures all things.

~The New Testament

Love may be symbolised by a triangle. The first angle is: love questions not. It is not a beggar.... Beggar's love is no love at all. The first sign of love is when love asks nothing, but gives everything.... The second angle of the triangle is that love knows no fear. You may cut me to pieces, and I will still love you.... The third angle of the love-triangle is that love is its own end. It can never be the means. The man who says, 'I love you for such and such a thing', does not love. Love can never be the means; it must be the perfect end.

~Swami Vivekananda

ANGER

When a person thinks about objects of desire,
it creates attachment.
From attachment arises desire, and desire
gives birth to anger.[4]
Anger gives rise to delusion, and from delusion
one loses memory.
Loss of memory destroys the capacity to discriminate
between good and evil,
and as a result of loss of discrimination,
one perishes.

~*The Bhagavad Gita*

Angry words and actions hurt oneself first and hurt oneself most of all.

~*Thich Nhat Hanh*

Usually when we are angry with someone, we are more interested in fighting with them than in taking care of our own feelings. It's like someone whose house is on fire running, after the person who has set fire to their

[4]Desire obstructed leads to anger.

house instead of going home to put out the flames. If we don't go home to take care of our anger, our whole house will burn down.

~Thich Nhat Hanh

You have heard that it was said to the ancient ones, 'You shall not murder' and 'Whoever murders will be in danger of the judgment'. But I tell you that everyone who is angry with his brother without a cause will be in danger of the judgment.

~The New Testament

Anger hurts the angered one more than
him who made him sore.
The fool who smites the ground smites
his hand the more.
The many tongues of anger's fire burn as the furies burn
so sense demands that you from anger turn.
Hold back that rage, hold it right back, for then you
gain not lose.
The tide on which your life's raft must cruise, those that
wrath burns up are as good as dead.
Who burn up their wrath are sages, no less, 'tis said.

~Kural

DESIRE

He who has discovered that there is no self,
will give up lust, desire, and egotism.

~The Buddha

There is no virtue in mere asceticism.
It is essential that you free yourself
from desire and attachment.
Give up desire, anger, greed and delusion,
and ask yourself, 'Who am I?'

~Adi Sankara

The mind of man is fickle.
He wants to fulfil all his desires, which is as likely as
filling a sieve with water.

~Mahavira

Desire is never extinguished by the enjoyment of objects
of desire; it only grows stronger as fire fed
with clarified butter.

~Manusmriti

The more one gets, the more one wants; with every gain, desire increases.

~*Uttaradhyayana Sutra*

As fire is covered by smoke, and mirror by dust, and as the womb is covered by the placenta, so is this (knowledge) covered by that (desire). Knowledge is concealed by the insatiable fire that is desire, which is forever the enemy of the man of wisdom.

~*The Bhagavad Gita*

One is to pray for desirelessness. For desire is the root cause of all suffering, and of birth, death and re-birth, and the obstacle to liberation.

~*Sri Sarada Devi*

The seed of seeds, say the wise,
is the thing called desire.
From which flow the twins, birth and death,
in a ceaseless gyre.
If it's desire that you desire it'll clasp and burn you in its fire And then you'll have to burn desire to flee its incinerating pyre.

~*Kural*

Do not desire, for what you desire you get,
and with it comes terrible bondage.

~Swami Vivekananda

Always without desire we must be found, if its deep
mystery we would sound;
but if desire always within us be,
its outer fringe is all that we shall see.

~Tao Te Ching

ATTACHMENT

The world is full of attachments, like a dream. As long as the attachment exists, it appears to be real, but it becomes unreal when one awakens to become aware of the realization of the Self.

~*Adi Sankara*

A person undoubtedly acquires flaws due to attachment of one's sense organs (to pleasure);
but by restraining them, one attains perfection.

~*Manusmriti*

It is because we mistakenly see ourselves as separate from everything else that we become attached.
If we fully appreciate that nothing is really separate to begin with, attachment becomes impossible.

~*Hazrat Sheikh Moinuddin Chishti*

Attachment and aversion are the root cause of karma[5].

~Mahavira

Non-attachment is that triumphant state of consciousness where there is absence of desire for objects that have been seen or heard of.

~Patanjali, Yoga Sutra

[5]The Indic notion of work which is bound by the cycle of cause and effect.

PRIDE

If you meet a sinner today
do not take pride in yourself.
Tomorrow, he might be on God's path while you might
have been distracted from it.
So never consider yourself
better than anyone you meet on this path.

~Hazrat Nizamuddin

That person is dear to all who is devoid of pride. Such a person acquires knowledge, fame, and wealth, and meets with success at every step.

~Bhagavati Aradhana

Greatness has no vanity.
And meanness no civility

~Kural

Pride, which is like a pillar of stone,
prevents a person from being humble
and drags the soul to hell.
One who humiliates others out of pride is ignorant.

~Mahavira

PRAISE AND REBUKE

As a rock that is a single mass is not moved by the wind, in the same way, a learned man is not shaken by censure or by praise.

~The Buddha

Only when I can withstand censure
Will my inhibitions break down.
Let my pride be torn asunder!
Let not attacks bother me!

~Lal Ded

EGO

Ego and possessiveness are terrible diseases;
it is a hindrance to life.

~Guru Granth Sahib

'I' and 'mine'—these two represent ignorance.

~Sri Ramakrishna

Pray to become selfless and see the path illuminate
before of you.

~Hazrat Nizamuddin

The eye that's glued to learning is blind to
the scripts of pain.
The ego just steamrolls the heart in
the service of the brain.
Have you ever felt pain as in 'felt' and in 'pain'? Yes?
Then you'll never give it to another,
not one dram or grain!

~Kural

Ego, greed, and lust waylay seekers of truth.
The one who triumphs over them and aspires only to serve is rid of all worldly attachments.

~Lal Ded

ENVY

Man makes the mistake of…identifying himself with the body.… This leads to inequality, which inevitably leads to struggle and jealousy.…

~Swami Vivekananda

Gripped by envy no man can move ahead.
He'll collapse under that load of lead.

~Kural

FEAR

Fear arises from the presence of another.

~Brihadaranyaka Upanishad

Fear is a worse disease than malaria or kalazar; these diseases kill the body, fear kills the soul.

~Mahatma Gandhi

If there is one word that you find coming out like a bomb from the Upanishads, bursting like a bomb-shell upon masses of ignorance, it is the word fearlessness [abhih].... Either in this world or in the world of religion, it is true that fear is the sure cause of degradation and sin. It is fear that brings misery, fear that brings death, fear that breeds evil.

~Swami Vivekananda

In enjoyment is the fear of disease;
in high birth, the fear of losing caste;
in wealth, the fear of tyrants;
in honour, the fear of losing her;
in strength, the fear of enemies;
in beauty, the fear of the other sex;
in knowledge, the fear of defeat;
in virtue, the fear of scandal;
in the body, the fear of death.
In this life, all is fraught with fear.
Renunciation alone is fearless.

~Bhartrihari's verses on renunciation
(translated by Swami Vivekananda)

IMPERMANENCE

The foundation of your life is but quicksand, your
attachments illusory. Hoard all that you wish,
you will have to leave it all behind.
Why then are you immersed in these things?

~Lal Ded

There is a tendency to believe that we will remain the same person forever, and that the person we are fighting with will remain the same person forever, that they will never change. This kind of delusion prevents us from living in a way that can bring happiness to ourself and to the other people.

~Thich Nhat Hanh

Do not worry if you are deprived
of all your worldly possessions.
They are transient.
The only permanence is the love of God.
Seek only that.

~Hazrat Nizamuddin

DEATH

Just as a cowherd drives cows to their destination with a rod, old age and death drive living beings.

~The Buddha

Chariots, thrones, pomp, and pleasure are forever, you think. Why then is the fear of death never far from you?

~Lal Ded

Every soul is infinite. Therefore there is no question of life and death.

~Swami Vivekananda

Our greatest fear is that when we die we will become nothing. To really be free of fear, we must look deeply into the ultimate dimension to see our true nature of no-birth and no-death. We need to free ourselves from these ideas that we are just our bodies, which die. When we understand that we are more than our physical bodies, that we didn't come from nothingness and will not disappear into nothingness, we are liberated from fear.

~Thich Nhat Hanh

Just as a person discards worn-out clothes and puts on other clothes that are new,
similarly, the in-dweller of the body discards bodies that are worn out, and acquires other bodies that are new.

~*The Bhagavad Gita*

The world is a place where nothing is lost: it is only changed.... Man does not lose his individuality after death. That personality is making his hereafter.

~*Hazrat Inayat Khan*

Death is not extinguishing the light.
It is only putting out the lamp
because the dawn has come.

~Rabindranath Tagore

It is as clear to me as daylight that life and death are but phases of the same thing, the reverse and obverse of the same coin.

~Mahatma Gandhi

First, there is pleasure, then there is disease.
Finally comes death.
Yet men do not give up their sinful ways.

~Adi Sankara

Keep handy all you need for the last journey—
a pure heart and good deeds.
And never forget that death is hovering over you
at all times.

~Hazrat Sheikh Moinuddin Chishti

LIFE

That I exist is a perpetual surprise which is life.

~Rabindranath Tagore

The noose of worldly life
is tightened by ignorance.
But illumined by the rays of pure consciousness,
you are truly liberated in life.

~Lal Ded

PAIN AND SUFFERING

Your pain is the breaking of the shell
that encloses your understanding.

~Kahlil Gibran

Pain is the hammer of the gods to break a dead
resistance in the mortal's heart.

~Sri Aurobindo

Deep suffering is calamitous,
like a lightning strike
and painful like being crushed in a flour mill.
It is despair like darkness at noon.
But suffer well, for suffering will lighten
the burden that is your ego.

~Lal Ded

Penance is about feeling another's pain as one's own.
And for any pain caused, quietly to atone.
To offer true penance you must know how to atone.
Else, be honest, stay as you are and leave penance alone.

~Kural

If a man speaks or acts with evil thoughts,
pain follows him like the wheel follows the foot of
the ox that draws the cart.

~The Buddha

Stay not with those who have never known
the ordeals of love. Live with those who have
surrendered to it and chosen to experience the pangs of
suffering with humility.

~Hazrat Nizamuddin

Both suffering and happiness are of an organic nature, which means they are both transitory; they are always changing. The flower, when it wilts, becomes the compost. The compost can help grow a flower again. Happiness is also organic and impermanent by nature. It can become suffering and suffering can become happiness again.

~Thich Nhat Hanh

Pleasure and pain are only aspects of the mind. Our essential nature is happiness, but we have forgotten the Self and imagine that the body or the mind is the Self. It is this wrong identification that gives rise to misery.

~Sri Ramana Maharshi

SIN

Arjuna said: Propelled by what, O Varshneya[7], does a human being commit sin, even if unwilling, as if driven by force?
Krishna said: It is desire, it is anger[8], that is born of *rajas*[9]. Unquenchable and intense, the cause of all sin, know it to be our enemy in this world.

~The Bhagavad Gita

Sin sinks our soul in more bondage.
Violence is a sin.
Theft is a sin.
Lying is a sin.
Destroying another life is a sin.
Even encouraging another.
To hurt others is a sin.

~Mahavira

---

[7]Another name for Krishna.

[8]Desire, when obstructed, turns into anger.

[9]Of the three qualities (sattva, rajas, and tamas), rajas represents anger, aggressiveness, activity, excessive pride, and egotism.

The person who says 'I am bound', 'I am bound' all the time, bound he becomes.

The one who repeats day and night 'I am a sinner', 'I am a sinner', he becomes a sinner.

~Sri Ramakrishna

Vedanta knows no sin. There are mistakes, but no sin; and in the long run everything is going to be all right. No Satan—none of this nonsense. Vedanta believes in only one sin, only one in the world, and it is this: the moment you think you are a sinner or anybody is a sinner, that is sin. From that follows every other mistake or what is usually called sin.

~Swami Vivekananda

SELF-CONTROL

Recognize and anticipate lust, anger, and greed,
and destroy them with good thoughts and
self-control. Or they will destroy you.

~Lal Ded

By extensively studying all learning, and keeping himself under the restraint of the rules of propriety, one may thus likewise not err from what is right.

~Confucius

Continence is of four kinds—of the mind,
body, speech, and possessions.

~Sthananga Sutra

PURITY

The sinner, like the deer hunter, bows down twice as much. What can be achieved by bowing the head, when the heart is impure?

~Guru Granth Sahib

One who is free of deceit is pure.
Only the pure attain liberation,
like a fire sprinkled with ghee.

~Mahavira

...the path of self-purification is hard and steep. To attain to perfect purity, one has to become absolutely passion-free in thought, speech, and action; to rise above the opposing currents of love and hatred, attachment, and repulsion.

~Mahatma Gandhi

A person of pure mind and heart becomes the
embodiment of the Divine on earth.
An act of charity in feeding the hungry creates seven
curtains between a person and hell.

~Hazrat Sheikh Moinuddin Chishti

Blessed are the pure in heart,
for they shall see God.

~The New Testament

'Blessed are the pure in heart, for they shall see God.'
This sentence alone would save mankind if all books
and prophets were lost.
This purity of heart will bring the vision of God....
In purity is no bondage.

~Swami Vivekananda

But few are those who tread the sunlit path;
only the pure in soul can walk in light.

~Sri Aurobindo

PRAYER

Sri Ramakrishna: God and His riches! This world represents His riches. But everybody gets swayed by His riches, they do not look for Him to whom it all belongs.

A *devotee*: What is the way out?

Sri Ramakrishna: The way out is holy company and prayer.

~Sri Ramakrishna

Prayer is a great necessity for the development of the soul.

~Hazrat Sheikh Moinuddin Chishti

GOOD AND EVIL

The flame of love will only kindle a heart that is pure and purged of any evil.

~Hazrat Nizamuddin

The mind encircled by evil, performs evil act.

~Guru Granth Sahib

Desire is the root of all evil;
hatred is the root of all evil;
delusion is the root of all evil.

~The Buddha

The root of evil is in the illusion that we are bodies. This, if any, is the original sin.

~Swami Vivekananda

This world is neither good nor evil; each man manufactures a world for himself. If a blind man begins to think of the world, it is either as soft or hard, or as cold or hot. We are a mass of happiness or misery; we have seen that hundreds of times in our lives.... Life is good or evil according to the state of mind in which we look at it, it is neither by itself. Fire, by itself, is neither good nor evil. When it keeps us warm we say, 'How beautiful is fire'. When it burns our fingers, we blame it. Still, in itself it is neither good nor bad. According as we use it, it produces in us the feeling of good or bad; so also is this world.

~Swami Vivekananda

RELIGION AND SPIRITUALITY

Religion is the manifestation of the
divinity already in man.

~Swami Vivekananda

If you can look at something and not covet it,
you have become spiritual.

~Swami Ashokananda

The essence of spirituality and mysticism is readiness to serve the person next to us.

~Hazrat Inayat Khan

Humanity is the greatest religion.
If you have a human approach,
you are a religious being.

~Hazrat Sheikh Moinuddin Chishti

Humanity is mind, not body—soul, not flesh.... To close against any the gates of the higher life is a sin far greater than that of murder, for it means responsibility for spiritual death, for inner bondage, and the result is ruin unspeakable.

~Sister Nivedita

I believe that prayer is the very soul and essence of religion, and therefore prayer must be the very core of life of man, for no man can live without religion...even a man who disowns religion cannot and does not live without religion.

~Mahatma Gandhi

No distinction, henceforth,
between sacred and secular.
To labour is to pray.
To conquer is to renounce.
Life is itself religion.

~Sister Nivedita

This is the gist of all worship—to be pure and to do good to others. He who sees Shiva[10] in the poor, in the weak, and in the diseased, really worships Shiva; and if he sees Shiva only in the image, his worship is but preliminary.

~Swami Vivekananda

True religion is defined by goodwill, love, truth, purity, nobility, and kindness.
All beings long for happiness; therefore, be compassionate towards all.

~The Buddha

The spiritual life…proceeds directly by a change of consciousness, a change from the ordinary consciousness, ignorant and separated from its true self and from God, to a greater consciousness in which one finds one's true being and comes first into direct and living contact and then into union with the Divine. For the spiritual seeker this change of consciousness is the one thing he seeks and nothing else matters.

~Sri Aurobindo

---

[10]The Hindu god, Shiva. This is an excerpt from a lecture delivered at the famous pilgrimage, Rameswaram, dedicated to Shiva.

DOING GOOD TO OTHERS

The loveless, wholly self-absorbed, in themselves stay mired. The loving, in their very bones, by care for others, are fired.

~Kural

They alone live who live for others. The rest are more dead than alive.

~Swami Vivekananda

Harsh judgments, arrogance, and divisive qualities are diluted in the river of our intentions to help others.

~Hazrat Sheikh Moinuddin Chishti

Even the least work done for others awakens the power within; even thinking the least good of others gradually instils into the heart the strength of a lion.

~Swami Vivekananda

One person's suffering represents the suffering of the world. If you can help one person, you help the whole world.

~Thich Nhat Hanh

The soul's natural progress is towards selflessness and purity.

~Mahatma Gandhi

SERVICE

The twin pillars of Sufism are selfless service and love. Only one who loves can serve.

~Hazrat Sheikh Moinuddin Chishti

Blessed are they whose bodies get destroyed in the service of others.

~Swami Vivekananda

Man's ultimate aim is the realization of God, and all his activities, social, political, religious, have to be guided by the ultimate aim of the vision of God. The immediate service of all human beings becomes a necessary part of the endeavour simply because the only way to find God is to see Him in His creation and be one with it. This can only be done by service of all.

~Mahatma Gandhi

If you wish to serve the Beloved (God),
you must serve others.
It is only in selfless service that
we see ourselves clearly.
The ego is smoothened, and we learn humility,
tenderness, and love.

~Hazrat Sheikh Moinuddin Chishti

To serve the world, looked upon as the manifestation of
the Lord, is to offer worship to the Lord of
the Eight Forms[11].

~Sri Ramana Maharshi

[11]Shiva

COMPASSION

To be kind, to care, and perhaps to love is to
have true wealth.
Even the vile have the other kind that rhymes so well
with 'stealth'.

~Kural

He who is loving and compassionate is able to give,
for he has banished hatred, envy, and anger.

~The Buddha

A person who is compassionate to
all living beings and whose love embraces the whole
universe gets auspicious karmas.

~Mahavira

He it is who trusteth away the orphan,
and stirreth not others up to feed the poor.
Woe to those who pray,
but in their prayer are careless;
who make a shew of devotion,
but refuse help to the needy.

~Quran

Compassionate listening and loving speech are doors that can help us out of even the most difficult situations. Once we have listened with compassion, we can use loving speech to restore communication and understanding.

~Thich Nhat Hanh

GENTLENESS

There is nothing in the world more soft and weak than water, and yet for attacking things that are firm and strong there is nothing that can take precedence of it—for there is nothing (so effectual) for which it can be changed. Everyone in the world knows that the soft overcomes the hard, and the weak the strong, but no one is able to carry it out in practice.

~*Tao Te Ching*

GIVING

You give but little when you give of your possessions.
It is when you give of yourself that you truly give.

~Kahlil Gibran

Feeding animals, watering plants, clearing the pathways of thorns and weeds—these too are acts of charity.

~Hazrat Sheikh Moinuddin Chishti

In the world take always the position of the giver. Give everything and look for no return. Give love, give help, give service, give any little thing you can, but keep out barter. Make no conditions, and none will be imposed.
Let us give out of our own bounty,
just as God gives to us.

~Swami Vivekananda

That gift which is given to a worthy recipient, at a right place and right time, without any expectation of return,
and with the feeling that it is a duty to give,
is called sattvika giving.
But that which is given in expectation of some return or benefit, and with a grudging attitude,
is called rajasika giving.
That gift which is made to an unworthy recipient, at an improper place and time, and with an attitude of disrespect and disdain,
is called tamasika giving[12].

~The Bhagavad Gita

When an object is given with due respect, at the right place and right time, following the right procedure, to a worthy recipient, it is all an unfailing sign of dharma[13].

~Yajnavalkya Smriti

One should give with reverence. One should not give disrespectfully. One should give in accordance with one's prosperity. One should give with modesty. One should give with awe. One should give in a friendly manner.

~Taittiriya Upanishad

---

[12]Sattvika, rajasika, and tamasika are the adjectival forms of the three qualities: sattva, rajas, and tamas, representing goodness, ego, and ignorance respectively.

[13]Right conduct.

... when you do merciful deeds, don't sound a trumpet before yourself, as the hypocrites do in the synagogues and in the streets, that they may get glory from men. Most certainly I tell you, they have received their reward. But when you do merciful deeds, don't let your left hand know what your right hand does, so that your merciful deeds may be in secret, then your Father who sees in secret will reward you openly.

~*The New Testament*

What's given to the needy is given from
one's giving purse.
What's 'given' otherwise is commerce.

~*Kural*

NON-INJURY

Considering all living beings as one's own self and working for the welfare of all living beings is called non-violence. It helps in achieving the knowledge of self.

~Linga Purana

...all religions have taught ethical precepts, such as, 'Do not kill, do not injure; love your neighbour as yourself,' etc.... Why should I not injure my neighbour... the Hindus say that this Atman is absolute and all-pervading, therefore infinite. There cannot be two infinites, for they would limit each other and would become finite. Also, each individual soul is a part and parcel of that Universal Soul, which is infinite. Therefore, in injuring his neighbour, the individual actually injures himself. This is the basic metaphysical truth underlying all ethical codes.

~Swami Vivekananda

Ahimsa is the eradication of the desire
to injure or to kill.

~*Mahatma Gandhi*

When one is firmly established in non-injury, all beings
in the vicinity cease to feel hostility.

~*Patanjali, Yoga Sutra*

TRUTH

Truth is the sole saviour of this world.
Truth is noble.

~Adi Sankara

One who is holding onto truth,
is lying in the lap of God.

~Sri Ramakrishna

Speak the truth, speak pleasantly, do not speak an unpleasant truth, and do not speak a pleasant falsehood; this is the eternal way[14].

~Manusmriti

Telling lies is like eating a dead body.

~Guru Granth Sahib

---

[14]The original expression is 'sanatana dharma', which means the Eternal Law or Righteousness.

Sufis march on the path of truth, practice truth to perfection, and shun falsehood to the core.

~Hazrat Sheikh Moinuddin Chishti

When we want to prove a point, we may be tempted to twist the truth or say something that is only partially true. We may exaggerate by intentionally making something out to be greater or more extreme than it is. We may add, embellish, or invent details to prove we are right. This kind of speech can lead to misunderstanding and distrust. We have to practice speaking the truth and speaking it skilfully. If we are not skilful, we may say something that we think is truthful but it might still make others suffer or despair.

~Thich Nhat Hanh

Retelling precisely what has been seen, heard, inferred, or experienced is called truthfulness (satya). It is devoid of injury or infliction of pain on others.

~Linga Purana

I will compare truth to a corrosive substance of infinite power. It burns its way in wherever it falls—in soft substance at once, hard granite slowly, but it must.

~Swami Vivekananda

Great is penance, greater still when it comes with charity. But greater far is truth in all its purity.

~Kural

When one is firmly established in truthfulness, action becomes fruitful.

~Patanjali, Yoga Sutra

For me, Truth is the sovereign principle, which includes numerous other principles. This truth is not only truthfulness in word, but truthfulness in thought also, and not only the relative truth of our conception, but the Absolute Truth, the Eternal principle, that is God.

~Mahatma Gandhi

RENUNCIATION

To enumerate the virtues of the venerated great,[15]
would be as tough as counting the dead.

~Kural

Tell me, Brother, how can I renounce Maya?
When I gave up the tying of ribbons,
still I tied my garment about me: when I gave up tying
my garment, still I covered my body in its folds.
So, when I give up passion, I see that anger remains;
and when I renounce anger, greed is with me still;
and when greed is vanquished, pride and vainglory
remain; when the mind is detached and casts Maya
away, still it clings to the letter. Kabir says, 'Listen to
me, dear Sadhu! the true path is rarely found.'

~Kabir (translated by Rabindranath Tagore)

He is a fakir who is indifferent to all worldly desires and does not want anything except the vision of God's eternal countenance because all creation is the mirror and reflection of that eternal countenance.

~Hazrat Sheikh Moinuddin Chishti

---

[15]In this context, it refers to ascetics and renunciates.

Give up, renounce the world. Now we are like dogs strayed into a kitchen and eating a piece of meat, looking round in fear lest at any moment someone may come and drive them out. Instead of that, be a king and know you own the world. This never comes until you give it up and it ceases to bind. Give up mentally, if you do not physically. Give up from the heart of your hearts.

~Swami Vivekananda

EQUANIMITY

O Partha[16], when, having given up all desires of the mind, one finds contentment within the Self alone, then one is called a person of steady wisdom.

Not perturbed by sorrow, past the longing for happiness, beyond attachment, fear, and anger, such a person is called a sage of steady wisdom.

One who is free from attachment to anything, who neither rejoices nor dislikes whatever good or evil he receives, is one whose wisdom is steady.

~*The Bhagavad Gita*

The man who gives way to anger, or hatred, or any other passion, cannot work; he only breaks himself to pieces, and does nothing practical. It is the calm, forgiving, equable, well-balanced mind that does the greatest amount of work.

~*Swami Vivekananda*

---

[16]Another name for Arjuna.

VIRTUE

Virtue confers honour and makes prosperity swell.
In the virtuous life alone does fortune dwell.

~*Kural*

Dharma[17] is that from which (results) the attainment of prosperity as well as liberation.

~*Vaisesika Sutra*

The first step to liberation is virtue.

~*Darsana Pahuda*

He who aims to be a man of complete virtue in his food does not seek to gratify his appetite, nor in his dwelling place does he seek the appliances of ease; he is earnest in what he is doing, and careful in his speech; he frequents the company of men of principle that he may be rectified—such a person may be said indeed to love to learn.

~*Confucius*

---

[17]Virtue.

Sweetness and humility, O Nanak, are the essence of virtue and goodness.

~Guru Granth Sahib

Closest to Allah is one who possesses the following three qualities: magnanimity of a river, kindness of the sun, and humility of the Earth.

~Hazrat Sheikh Moinuddin Chishti

The eight virtues of the self are: compassion for all creatures, forbearance, lack of envy, purity, tranquillity, an auspicious disposition, generosity, and non-covetousness.

~Gautama Dharmasutra

Dharma[18] that is common to all are: non-injury, truthfulness, purity, lack of malice, compassion, and forbearance.

~Arthasastra

---

[18]Duty.

Moral conduct consists of non-injury, truthfulness, not stealing, chastity, and non-acquisitiveness. These great vows are universal and not affected by birth, place, time, and conventions.

~Patanjali, Yoga Sutra

The gateways to virtue are fourfold—forgiveness, contentment, simplicity, and modesty.

~Sthananga Sutra

HUMILITY

Everyone wants others to bow down to him; no one bows to the other. Find out, weighing in the weigh scale, one that bows down is heavier.

~Guru Granth Sahib

We come nearest to the great
when we are great in humility.

~Rabindranath Tagore

HOSPITALITY

Grain'll ripen unsown on your field
if your guest you welcome make.
And only after he's eaten, of what remains, partake.

~*Kural*

A guest who arrives in the evening should not be turned away, but be greeted with pleasant words, a place (to sit) on the floor, some straw, and water.

~*Yajnavalkya Smriti*

BEAUTY

It is useless to try and put into words what beauty is; but if anything can explain it, it is the other word for beauty, and that is harmony.... In order to be beautiful an object must be harmonious, for in point of fact harmony is beauty.

~Hazrat Inayat Khan

All in the world know the beauty of the beautiful, and in doing this they have (the idea of) what ugliness is; they all know the skill of the skilful, and in doing this they have (the idea of) what the want of skill is.

~Tao Te Ching

WEALTH

Those who make righteous use of money, such as in service to God, service rendered to monks and devotees, and charity, money serves some purpose only for them.

~Sri Ramakrishna

Do not accumulate what you do not need.
The excess of wealth in your hands is for society, and you are its trustee.

~Mahavira

Woe to every Backbiter, Defamer!
Who amasseth wealth and storeth it against the future!
He thinketh surely that his wealth shall be with him for ever.

~Quran

No servant can serve two masters, for either he will hate the one and love the other; or else he will hold to one and despise the other.
You cannot faithfully serve both God and money.

~The New Testament

WORK

To work you have the right, not to the fruits thereof;
be not the cause of fruits of action,
nor be inclined to inaction.
Work, O Dhananjaya[19], while being established in Yoga[20], giving up attachment [to fruits of action], and considering success and failure to be same; this state of sameness is called Yoga[21].

~The Bhagavad Gita

The fruits of action are not everlasting, and they cause one to fall into the great ocean of *karma*[22], blocking spiritual progress. The action which is done without personal desire and whose fruits are surrendered to the Lord, purifies the mind and leads to liberation.

~Sri Ramana Maharshi

---

[19]Another name of Arjuna.

[20]Union with God or the Ultimate Truth.

[21]One who can practice sameness of vision is able to remain unruffled, which is indispensable for Yoga; sameness of vision also means one is able to see the Ultimate Truth that is beyond the duality of good and evil.

[22]The incessant cycle of cause and effect produced by action.

All work is by nature composed of good and evil. We cannot do any work which will not do some good somewhere; there cannot be any work which will not cause some harm somewhere. Every work must necessarily be a mixture of good and evil; yet we are commanded to work incessantly. Good and evil will both have their results, will produce their karma. Good action will entail upon us good effect; bad action, bad. But good and bad are both bondages of the soul. The solution reached in the Gita in regard to this bondage-producing nature of work is that, if we do not attach ourselves to the work we do, it will not have any binding effect on our soul.

~Swami Vivekananda

There can be no Karmayoga[23] without the will to get rid of ego, rajas, and desire, which are the seals of ignorance

~Sri Aurobindo

Be patient: if the pen inscribing your accomplishments is slow and sluggish, it means that your work is still incomplete. Persevere on the path.

~Hazrat Nizamuddin

---

[23]The method of using Karma or work as a means of spiritual development.

He who works with respect for the work, not driven by desire, will do well—be he king, be he clerk.

~*Kural*

FREEDOM

...freedom is the first condition of growth. What you do not make free, will never grow.

~*Swami Vivekananda*

Once we know that 'I' am not my physical body, but a soul trapped within this body, we truly begin the path to freedom. Such freedom is bliss!

~*Mahavira*

The 'I', the 'I' and 'my' and 'mine' are weightless weight
That shed fast will take you through freedom's gate.

~*Kural*

KNOWLEDGE

The wise one does not know many things; one who knows many things is not wise.

~*Tao Te Ching*

One may go to the Ganga and to different oceans for a dip, one may do penance and charity,
but people who do not have right knowledge and mindlessly repeat these rituals assuming that they alone will help them, they can never get liberation, irrespective of which religion they may belong to.

~*Adi Sankara*

Just as a threaded needle does not get lost even when it falls, a person endowed with spiritual knowledge does not get destroyed even in the maze of worldly life.

~*Uttaradhyayana Sutra*

The cause of all the miseries we have in the world is that men foolishly think pleasure to be the ideal to strive for. After a time man finds that it is not happiness, but knowledge, towards which he is going, and that both pleasure and pain are great teachers, and that he learns as much from evil as from good.

~Swami Vivekananda

What is knowledge?
Knowledge is to know one's real nature, that is pure atman, and to contemplate on it.

~Sri Ramakrishna

That which helps to understand the truth, that which helps to control the mind, and that which purifies the soul, is Knowledge.

~Mulachara

What the soul sees and has experienced, that it knows; the rest is appearance, prejudice, and opinion.

~Sri Aurobindo

Knowledge of the heart preferable to the knowledge of the schools. The knowledge of men of heart bears them up, the knowledge of men of the body weighs them

down. When 'tis knowledge of the heart, it is a friend; when knowledge of the body, it is a burden. God saith, 'As an ass bearing a load of books,' the knowledge which is not of Him is a burden.
Knowledge which comes not immediately from Him endures no longer than the rouge of the tirewoman.

~Rumi

The one possessing shraddha,[24] ever eager, and with all sense organs under restraint, attains Knowledge.

~The Bhagavad Gita

No knowledge comes from outside; it is all inside. What we say a man 'knows', should, in strict psychological language, be what he 'discovers' or 'unveils'; what a man 'learns' is really what he 'discovers', by taking the cover off his own soul, which is a mine of infinite knowledge.

~Swami Vivekananda

---

[24]Shraddha means faith; it is not ordinary belief, but faith in something whose truth has already been established. Shraddha denotes an openness or a positive attitude towards receiving knowledge.

FAITH

It is faith that steers us through stormy seas, faith that moves mountains and faith that jumps across the ocean. That faith is nothing but a living, wide-awake consciousness of God within. He who has achieved that faith wants nothing.

~Mahatma Gandhi

Faith is the bird that feels the light and sings when the dawn is still dark.

~Rabindranath Tagore

Live before you die.
Be present in every moment and have deep gratitude for life. The faithful do not die, they transcend from this perishable world to the world of eternal existence.

~Hazrat Sheikh Moinuddin Chishti

STRENGTH

Strength, strength is what the Upanishads speak to me from every page. This is the one great thing to remember, it has been the one great lesson I have been taught in my life; strength, it says, strength, O man, be not weak. Are there no human weaknesses?—says man. There are, say the Upanishads, but will more weakness heal them, would you try to wash dirt with dirt? Will sin cure sin, weakness cure weakness? Strength, O man, strength, say the Upanishads, stand up and be strong.

~Swami Vivekananda

Greatness of mind is always meek and humble; but cruelty is a note and an effect of weakness, and brings down a governor to the level of a competitor.

~Seneca

The great are strongest when they stand alone.

~Sri Aurobindo

REASON

A mind all logic is like a knife all blade. It makes the hand bleed that uses it.

~Rabindranath Tagore

Your reason and your passion are the rudder and the sails of your seafaring soul.

If either your sails or your rudder be broken, you can but toss and drift, or else be held at a standstill in mid seas. For reason, ruling alone, is a force confining; and passion, unattended, is a flame that burns to its own destruction. Therefore let your soul exalt your reason to the height of passion, that it may sing; and let it direct your passion with reason, that your passion may live through its own daily resurrection, and like the phoenix rise above its own ashes.

~Kahlil Gibran

THE SELF

The soul is called Atman, which means happiness or bliss itself. It is not that happiness belongs to the soul; it is that the soul itself is happiness.

~Hazrat Inayat Khan

Every soul is omniscient and blissful from within. The bliss does not come from outside.

~Mahavira

It is said that all these bodies are subject to destruction, while the one[25] who resides in the body is eternal, indestructible and imperceptible.

~The Bhagavad Gita

The soul is eternal.
Neither was it created nor can it be destroyed.

~Mahavira

---

[25]Atman

One who knows the self to be wholly different from the impure body and to be the knower of all substances, knows the essence of all scriptures.

~Kartikeyanupreksa

The Self is free from the activities of mind, body, and speech. It is devoid of conflict, formless, without substratum, unattached, without blemish, and free from delusion and fear.

~Niyama Sara

The soul comes alone and goes alone.
Nobody accompanies it,
and nobody becomes its mate.

~Mahavira

The Self is neither the body nor the mind, neither speech, nor their cause. It is neither the doer, nor the cause of action, nor the approver of any action.

~Pravachana Sara

In the mind that is stable like
the water of a clear pond.
The reflection of the Self can be seen.

~Tattva Sara

Everyone is the Self and, indeed, is infinite. Yet each person mistakes his body for his Self... Once the false notion 'I am the body'...has been removed, the Supreme Consciousness or the Self alone remains....

~Sri Ramana Maharshi

When the Self is seen existing as distinct [from nature, activities of the mind, and everything else with which it is generally identified], all causes [of further creation] come to an end.

~Patanjali, Yoga Sutra

BODY AND MIND

…the greatest of all lies is that we are bodies, which we never were nor even can be.

~Swami Vivekananda

Believing yourself to be your body,
you stayed entangled in its affairs.
You indulged it without end. But it won't last,
not even ashes or its smell.

~Lal Ded

Misguided by the idea that the physical body is 'Me', we carry the burden of the body and everything we possess. We cannot experience freedom as long as we carry this burden. True freedom is freedom from this burden.

~Mahavira

The finer the instrument, the greater the power. The mind is much finer and more powerful than the body.

~Swami Vivekananda

The mind commands the body, and it obeys instantly; the mind commands itself, and is resisted.

~Saint Augustine

The mind-stallion races all over the skies.
In a moment it crosses a hundred thousand leagues.
Seize it! Bind it!
And leash it with your breath, bringing poise and ease to yourself.

~Lal Ded

Five are the afflictions of the mind:
ignorance; egotism; attachment; aversion;
and the fear of death....
Ignorance is considering the impermanent, impure,
suffering non-self as the Self,
which is in reality, eternal, pure, and blissful.
Egotism is conflating the power of the seer
(pure consciousness) with the power of
perception all by itself.
Attachment follows the experience of pleasure.
Aversion follows the experience of pain
And the fear of death, that is, the will to live, is deep-rooted, and flows spontaneously even in the learned....
These tendencies can be discarded through meditation.

~Patanjali, Yoga Sutra

Depth in meditation will not come without quieting the mind. The mind is quieted best by unselfishness—there is no technique so good!

~Swami Ashokananda

The mind radiates serenity when it cultivates friendliness toward the pleasant, compassion toward the unhappy, joy in the meritorious, and indifference toward the unmeritorious.

~Patanjali, Yoga Sutra

It is only when the mind is under control that attachment and aversion—the causes of worldly suffering—can be destroyed.

~Bhagavati Aradhana

What one has thought of as his mind is merely a bundle of thoughts. All these thoughts depend upon the one thought of 'I', the ego. Therefore, the so-called mind is the 'I' thought.

~Sri Ramana Maharshi

The mad elephant is controlled and held captive by the chains; so is the unstable mind controlled and held captive by the chains of knowledge.

~Bhagavati Aradhana

Control of the mind is perfected when it is free from inauspicious thoughts and full of auspicious thoughts.

~Dasavaikalika-Churni

FOOD AND EATING

Food when eaten becomes divided into three parts. The grossest part thereof becomes excreta. That which is the medium constituent becomes flesh. That which is the subtlest part becomes mind.

~*Chandogya Upanishad*

Health has much to do with what and when and how you eat. Let what's inside you settle before you pile more and more on't.

~*Kural*

Those who have not amassed wealth, those who recognize the value of food, whose goal is liberation from this void without any special purpose, their movement is hard to trace like that of birds in the sky.

~*The Buddha*

WORDS

Oh dear, one should not speak in a way
that hurts others!
Even if what you say is true, it should not be spoken in
a hurtful way.

~Sri Sarada Devi

In my opinion the Sanskrit text 'satyam bruyat priyam bruyat, na bruyat satyam apriyam'[26] means that one should speak the truth in gentle language. One had better not speak it, if one cannot do so in a gentle way; meaning thereby that there is no truth in a man who cannot control his tongue.

~Mahatma Gandhi

Words can slice the heart, split open the brain.
They can make friends vanish
and leave you in lonely pain.

~Kural

---

[26]'Speak the truth, speak pleasantly, do not speak an unpleasant truth.'

If you speak kind words and encourage them, they are bound to improve in time.
If you can give them positive ideas, people will grow up to be men and learn to stand on their own legs.

~ *Swami Vivekananda*

Better than a thousand useless words is a single useful sentence.

~ *The Buddha*

EDUCATION

To me the very essence of education is concentration of mind, not the collecting of facts. If I had to do my education over again, and had any voice in the matter, I would not study facts at all. I would develop the power of concentration and detachment, and then with a perfect instrument I could collect facts at will. Side by side, in the child, should be developed the power of concentration and detachment.

~Swami Vivekananda

The first principle of true teaching is that nothing can be taught.

~Sri Aurobindo

Bodily exercise, when compulsory, does no harm to the body; but knowledge which is acquired under compulsion obtains no hold on the mind.

~Plato

Our conception of education must have a soul. It must form a unity. It must take note of the child as a whole, as heart as well as mind, will as well as mind and heart. Unless we train the *feelings* and the *choice*, our man is not educated.

~Sister Nivedita

An education which does not teach us to discriminate between good and bad, to assimilate the one and eschew the other, is a misnomer.

~Mahatma Gandhi

Don't limit a child to your own learning,
for she was born in another time.

~Rabindranath Tagore

What then have I to do with men, that they should hear my confessions—as if they could heal all my infirmities—a race, curious to know the lives of others, slothful to amend their own?

~Saint Augustine

The only remedy for bad habits is counter habits; all the bad habits that have left their impressions are to be controlled by good habits. Go on doing good, thinking holy thoughts continuously; that is the only way to suppress base impressions. Never say any man is hopeless, because he only represents a character, a bundle of habits, which can be checked by new and better ones. Character is repeated habits, and repeated habits alone can reform character.

~Swami Vivekananda

We have the seeds, the potential in us for understanding, love, compassion, and insight, as well as the seeds of anger, hate, and greed. While we can't avoid all suffering in life, we can suffer much less by not watering the seeds of suffering inside us.

~Thich Nhat Hanh

Anger spoils good relations, pride destroys humility, deceit destroys friendship, and greed destroys everything.

~Dasavaikalika Sutra

Speak the truth. Practice righteousness. Make no mistake about study.... Let your mother be god to you. Let your father be god to you. Let your teacher be god to you. Let a guest be god to you....

~Taittiriya Upanishad

The superior man wishes to be slow in his speech and earnest in his conduct.

~Confucius

Excessive indulgence will do you no good.
Excessive abstention will breed pride.
Stay the middle course and eat but little.
Moderation will open all doors.

~Lal Ded

There is no quality that equals forbearance. The one who endures is the one who outlasts.

~Sri Ramakrishna

God grows weary of great kingdoms,
but never of little flowers.

~Rabindranath Tagore

When we are visited with sickness or other afflictions we are not to murmur as if we were ill-used—it is a mark of the general's esteem when he puts us upon a post of danger: we do not say 'My captain uses me ill,' but 'he does me honor;' and so should we say that are commanded to encounter difficulties, for this is our case with God Almighty.

~Seneca

If you shed tears when you miss the sun,
you also miss the stars.

~Rabindranath Tagore

This one is my kin and that one a stranger—those who discriminate in this manner are people with petty minds. People with evolved consciousness embrace the entire world as their own family.

~Maha Upanishad

...there are three aspects, three principles in life: Jelal, Jemal, and Kemal. Jelal is power, Jemal is beauty, and Kemal is perfection...the third aspect is Kemal; no action is needed there. One has to be quiet, one has to be meditative, one has to be silent, one has to close one's eyes and get in touch with one's self within....

~*Hazrat Inayat Khan*

ACKNOWLEDGEMENTS

Grateful acknowledgement is made to the following copyright holders for permission to reprint copyrighted material in this volume:

Aphorisms by Hazrat Inayat Khan and from the Linga Purana reprinted by the permission of Motilal Banarsidass Publishing House.

Aphorisms by Ramana Maharshi reprinted by the permission of Sri Ramanasramam.

Aphorisms by Sister Nivedita reprinted by the permission of Advaita Ashrama, from the following sources:

Paper on Education-II, Hints on National Education in India, *Collected Works of Sister Nivedita (CWSN)*, Vol. 4, pp. 342–343.

Our Master and His Message, Introduction to Complete Works of Swami Vivekananda, *CWSN*, Vol. 1, p. 9

Paper on Education-III, Hints on National Education in India, *CWSN*, Vol. 4, p. 344.

Aphorisms by Swami Ashokananda reprinted by the permission of Kalpa Tree Press.

Aphorisms by Adi Sankara from '*You Are the Supreme Light': Life Lessons from Adi Shankara* edited by Nanditha Krishna. Reprinted by the permission of the editor.

Aphorisms by the Buddha from '*See Things As They Are': Life Lessons from the Buddha* edited by Nanditha Krishna.

Reprinted by the permission of the editor.

Aphorisms by Mahavira from *'Live and Let Others Live': Life Lessons from Mahavira* edited by Nanditha Krishna. Reprinted by the permission of the editor.

Aphorisms by Hazrat Nizamuddin from *'One Who Serves Becomes the Master': Life Lessons from Hazrat Nizamuddin* edited by Bela Upadhyay. Reprinted by the permission of the editor.

Aphorisms by Lal Ded from *'Looking Within': Life Lessons from Lal Ded* translated and edited by Shonaleeka Kaul. Reprinted by the permission of the translator and editor.

Aphorisms by Hazrat Sheikh Moinuddin Chishti from *'Be Present in Every Moment': Life Lessons from Moinuddin Chishti* edited by Babli Parveen. Reprinted by the permission of the editor.